Restaurant Copycat Recipes

Easy And Delicious Dishes To Prepare At Home From Your Favorite Restaurant

Sommario

Introduction

Every so often, you dig into a restaurant's food and comment on how it is so delicious that you can eat it everyday. While frequenting a specific restaurant just to eat your favorite dish is great for the owner's business, it can be damaging to your finances and very inconvenient, especially if the establishment isn't located near you.

Now all this won't be a problem anymore, in this book I want to give you all the exact ingredients of your favorite restaurants and dishes, so let's get ready to start...

Chapter 1: Breakfast

Porto's Guava Cheese Strudel

Preparation Time: 10 minutes

Cooking time: 45 minutes

Servings: 8

Ingredients:

Egg wash

1 egg, beaten

1 tablespoon water

Strudel

1 tablespoon powdered sugar

1 box frozen puff pastry dough, thawed

1 (8-ounce) package cream cheese

1 (8-ounce) package guava paste or guayabate 1 tablespoon coarse sugar

Directions:

Preheat oven to 400°F. Line a baking sheet.

Prepare the egg wash. Whisk the egg and water together in a small bowl. Set aside.

Dust work surface with powdered sugar.

Unfold pastry over powdered sugar.

Cut pastry into 12 squares and place on lined baking sheet.

Top 6 pastry squares with about a tablespoon each of guava paste and a tablespoon each of cream cheese.

Brush the edges with egg wash.

Cut 4 short slits in the centers of the remaining pastry squares.

Cover the filled squares, pressing down at the edges to seal.

Bake until puffed and golden brown (about 20 minutes).

Remove from oven and let cool on baking sheets for 3–5 minutes.

Transfer to wire rack to cool completely.

Sawmill Gravy and Biscuits

Preparation Time: 10 minutes

Cooking time: 45 minutes

Servings: 8

Ingredients:

¼ cup sausage patty grease

¼ cup flour

1 sausage patty

½ cup bacon bits

2 cups milk

½ teaspoon salt

½ teaspoon coarsely ground pepper

Buttermilk biscuits for serving

Directions:

Add the sausage patty to a skillet and cook through. Remove from skillet and allow to cool, then crumble.

Add the flour to the grease from the sausage in the skillet and stir until well combined.

Add the milk and cook while whisking constantly to avoid burning the milk. The gravy will thicken and bubble. Add the salt and pepper, crumbled sausage, and bacon bits.

Serve with your favorite buttermilk biscuits.

If you want to make a large batch of this gravy, you can use breakfast sausage chubs instead of a patty and crumble while you cook, then remove from the skillet and prepare the gravy the same way. You will need to increase the other ingredients proportionately, of course.

Starbucks' Spinach and Feta Breakfast Wraps

Preparation Time: 10 minutes

Cooking time: 45 minutes

Servings: 8

Ingredients:

10 ounces spinach leaves

1 14½-ounce can diced tomatoes, drained

3 tablespoons cream cheese

10 egg whites

½ teaspoon oregano

½ teaspoon garlic salt

⅛ teaspoon pepper

6 whole wheat tortillas

4 tablespoons feta cheese, crumbled

Cooking Spray

Directions:

Apply light coating of cooking spray to a pan. Cook spinach leaves on medium-high heat for 5 minutes or until leaves wilt, then stir in tomatoes and cream cheese. Cook for an additional 5 minutes or until cheese is melted completely. Remove from pan and place into glass bowl and cover. Set aside.

In the same pan, add egg whites, oregano, salt, and pepper. Stir well and cook at least 5 minutes or until eggs are scrambled. Remove from heat.

Microwave tortillas for 30 seconds or until warm. Place egg whites, spinach and tomato mixture, and feta in the middle of the tortillas. Fold sides inwards, like a burrito.

Serve.

Blueberry Syrup

Preparation Time: 10 minutes

Cooking time: 20 minutes

Servings: 8

Ingredients:

2 cups blueberries

½ cup sugar

1 cup water

1 tablespoon cornstarch

Directions:

Combine the cornstarch with 2 tablespoons of water in a small bowl. Whisk until no longer clumpy and set aside.

Combine the water, blueberries and sugar in a saucepan. Bring the mixture to a boil, then reduce the heat and simmer for about 10 minutes or until it has reduced a bit. Stir in the cornstarch and whisk until well combined. Continue to simmer and stir until the sauce has thickened.

When it has reached a syrup-like consistency, remove from heat. You can mix with an immersion blender if you choose.

Serve with pancakes or waffles.

Cracker Barrel Fried Apples

Preparation Time: 10 minutes

Cooking time: 20 minutes

Servings: 8

Ingredients:

8 red apples

½ cup sugar

¼ pound butter

Dash of nutmeg

1 teaspoon cinnamon

Directions:

1. Do not peel the apples. Slice the apples into ½" thick slices.

2. Melt butter over medium, in a nonstick pan.

3. Fill the skillet with apples and sugar.

4. Cover the skillet with a lid and cook for 20 minutes, or until the apples are tender and juicy.

5. Until serving sprinkle with cinnamon and nutmeg.

Chapter 2: Appetizers

Chili's Cheddar Cheese Bites

Preparation Time: 10 minutes

Cooking Time: 10 minutes

Servings: 12

Ingredients:

1 pound cubed cheddar cheese or cheese curds

1 ¼ cups all-purpose flour, divided

1 cup beer

Oil, as required for deep-fat frying

Directions:

Place ¼ cup of the flour in a large re-sealable plastic bag. Slowly add in the cheese curds & shake until nicely coated.

Now, over moderate heat in a deep fryer or an electric skillet; heat the oil. In the meantime, whisk the beer with leftover flour in a large bowl. Slowly dip the cheese curds into the batter & fry until turn golden brown, for 2 to 3 minutes per side. Place them on paper towels to drain.

Aunt Annie's Pretzels

Preparation Time: 15 minutes

Cooking Time: 25 minutes

Servings: 4

Ingredients:

2 -4 tablespoons melted butter

3 cups all-purpose flour

1 cup bread flour

2 tablespoons baking soda

1 ¼ teaspoons salt

2 tablespoons brown sugar

1 package active dry yeast (1 ¼ teaspoons)

2 cups water

1 ½ cups water

Coarse salt

Directions:

Pour lukewarm water in a large sized mixing bowl & then sprinkle the yeast on top of it; stir several times until completely dissolved.

Add sugar and salt; stir several times until dissolved and then add in the flour; knead dough for couple of minutes, until smooth & elastic. Leave everything for a minimum period of half an hour and let it rise.

While the dough is rising, mix 2 tablespoons of baking soda with 2 cups of warm water; stir often. After half an hour, pinch the dough bits off & roll into a ½" thick long rope & shape.

Dip the pretzel into the soda solution; placing it on a baking sheet, lightly greased. Let the pretzels to rise for a second time. Bake in the oven until turns golden, for 10 minutes, at 450 F. Brush the baked pretzel with the melted butter. After brushing; sprinkle with the coarse salt.

For Auntie Anne's famous Cinnamon Sugar: make a mixture of cinnamon and sugar in a large sized shallow bowl and melt a butter stick in a separate shallow bowl.

First dip the pretzel in butter, make sure both sides of the pretzel are generously coated with the melted butter & then dip once again into the cinnamon mixture.

Olive Garden Stuffed Mushrooms

Preparation Time: 10 minutes
Cooking time: 25 minutes
Servings: 8

Ingredients:

½ teaspoon of minced fresh parsley

2 to 3 slices of mozzarella cheese

2 tablespoons of minced red bell pepper

3 tablespoons of butter, melted

12 medium white button mushrooms with their stems removed

3 tablespoons of chicken broth

½ teaspoon of minced garlic

1 tablespoon of shredded Romano cheese

1 tablespoon of shredded Parmesan cheese

¼ cup of canned minced clams (make sure you drain the liquid)

⅓ cup of Progresso breadcrumbs (herb flavor)

Directions:

1) Prepare the oven by preheating it to 450 degrees F.

2) In a medium bowl, mix the Romano cheese, garlic, Parmesan cheese, clams, and breadcrumbs. Mix them well with your hands, then add the chicken broth 1

tablespoon at a time and stir well with a spoon after each addition.

3) Fill each mushroom cap with 1 to 2 teaspoons of stuffing. Make sure to keep the surface flat to support the sliced cheese.

4) Place the mushrooms in a pan (with baking paper on it) with the stuffing side facing up.

5) Brush melted butter over each mushroom, and pour the remaining melted butter into the dish.

6) Add minced red bell pepper on top of the stuffed mushrooms, then place the cheese slices on top. Make sure that the stuffing is covered.

7) Let the mushrooms bake for about 12 to 15 minutes, or until the cheese turns golden brown.

8) When the mushrooms are ready, take them out of the oven and sprinkle ½ teaspoon of minced parsley on top to serve.

Chili's Boneless Buffalo Wings

Preparation Time: 10 minutes

Cooking time: 50 minutes

Servings: 8

Ingredients:

¼ cup hot sauce

½ teaspoon ground pepper

2 teaspoons salt

¼ teaspoon cayenne pepper

¼ teaspoon paprika

1 cup flour

1 egg

2 boneless skinless chicken breasts

1 cup milk

2-4 cups cooking oil

1 tablespoon margarine

Directions:

1. Combine salt, peppers, flour, and paprika in a medium bowl.

2. In another bowl whisk the egg and milk together.

3. Cut each chicken breast into bite-size portions.

4. Preheat oil in skillet or deep fryer.

5. Dip the pieces of the chicken into the mixture of the eggs 1 or 2 at a time, then into the mixture of flour / spice. Repeat to double coating per piece of chicken.

6. Once all the pieces of chicken are breaded, place them on a plate and chill for 15 minutes.

7. Drop each chicken piece into hot oil and fry for 5-6 minutes or until golden brown is cooked.

8. Blend the margarine and hot sauce in a small, microwave-safe dish. Microwave for about 20-30 minutes or until the margarine has melted.

9. Upon frying, remove the chicken pieces to a plate lined with paper towels to absorb the excess oil.

10. Place the pieces of chicken inside a sealed dish. Pour the sauce over the chicken, put on the lid and gently shake until each piece of chicken is covered with sauce.

Olive Garden Bruschetta

Preparation Time: 10 minutes

Cooking time: 55 minutes

Servings: 8

Ingredients:

Pinch of dried parsley flakes

1 tablespoon of grated Parmesan cheese

9 to 10 slices of ciabatta bread

¼ teaspoon of salt

1 teaspoon of balsamic vinegar

2 teaspoons of extra virgin olive oil

2 teaspoons of diced marinated sun-dried tomatoes

2 teaspoons of minced garlic

1 tablespoon of minced fresh basil

3 firm Roma tomatoes, finely diced (it should be about 1 ½ cups)

Directions:

1) Use a medium bowl to mix the garlic, basil, sun-dried tomatoes, olive oil, vinegar, tomatoes, and salt. Mix well, cover and then let it chill for about an hour.

2) Prepare the oven by preheating it to 450 degrees.

3) Use a small bowl to mix dried parsley with Parmesan cheese. Place the bread slices on a tray with a baking sheet on it. Sprinkle the Parmesan cheese mixture on

each slice, and bake for about 5 minutes, or until the bread becomes crispy.

4) Take the bread slices out of the oven, put the tomato mixture into a serving dish, and serve alongside the bread slices.

Tip: When you put the tomatoes in a serving dish, be sure to drain the liquid.

Chapter 3: Salads and Side Dishes

Chicken BBQ Salad

Preparation time: 40 minutes

Cooking Time: 15 minutes

Serving: 4

Ingredients:

1 large boneless, skinless chicken breast

3 tablespoon ranch dressing

1 can of black beans

Large head of romaine lettuce

1 cup of corn kernels, fresh or frozen

3 tablespoon barbecue sauce plus more for marinating and drizzling

1 cup tri-color tortilla strips

Directions:

Place the chicken breast in a large zip-lock bag & add in the barbecue sauce; enough to cover the meat. Seal & let marinate for half an hour.

Preheat your grill over medium high heat.

Rinse the black beans, chop the romaine lettuce & heat a grill pan over medium high heat.

For dressing: Combine barbecue sauce together with ranch to taste.

Spray the grill with non-stick grilling spray & place the marinated chicken breast over the grill. Grill until the chicken is completely cooked through & juices run clear, for six minutes per side.

In the meantime, add corn to the grill pan. Lightly sprinkle with smoked paprika & grill until a few kernels are blackened slightly.

Let the chicken to rest for a few minutes and then dice into small bite-sized pieces.

Add romaine together with chicken, black beans, tortilla strips and corn in a large serving bowl. Add dressing; toss until evenly coated. Drizzle more of barbecue sauce on top of the ingredients, if desired. Serve immediately & enjoy.

Hooters Pasta Salad

Preparation Time: 20 minutes

Cooking Time: 30 minutes

Servings: 4

Ingredients:

1 ½ tablespoon granulated sugar

⅓ cup red wine vinegar

2 teaspoon minced shallot

½ teaspoon thyme, dried

1 teaspoon lemon juice, fresh

⅔ cup vegetable oil

¼ teaspoon parsley flakes, dried

1 tablespoon Grey Poupon Dijon mustard

¼ teaspoon garlic powder

A pinch of onion powder

⅛ teaspoon each of salt, coarsely ground black pepper, dried basil & dried oregano

4 quarts water

1 pound tri color radiatore or raindbow rotini (red, green and white color)

2 medium or 1 large tomatoes

1 green onion

¼ cup cucumber, minced

Salt to taste

1 to 2 teaspoon vegetable oil

Green leaf lettuce, for garnish, optional

Directions:

For Dressing: Combine granulated sugar together with red wine vinegar, minced shallot, thyme, lemon juice, vegetable oil, parsley flakes, Grey Poupon Dijon mustard, garlic powder, onion powder, salt, coarsely ground black pepper, dried basil & dried oregano using an electric mixer in a large bowl. Continue to mix on high speed until the dressing becomes thick & creamy, for a minute or two. Put the prepared dressing to a sealed container and store in a refrigerator until ready to toss.

Fill a deep pot with 4 quarts of water and bring it to a boil. Once done; add the pasta & cook until tender, for 12 to 15 minutes; drain well.

Spray a gentle stream of cold water over the hot pasta. Drizzle with the oil and gently toss. Add it in the covered container and let cool for 30 minutes in a refrigerator.

In the meantime; prepare the vegetables. Remove the soft pulp and seeds from the tomatoes before dicing, use the green part of scallions or green onion and mince the cucumber into small pieces.

When you can handle the pasta easily; add the diced tomato with cucumber and green onion. Sprinkle salt over the pasta salad and place it in the refrigerator again until chilled well.

When done; spoon it over the plates & place the prepared vinaigrette dressing on the side

Brussels Sprouts N' Kale Salad

Preparation Time: 5 minutes

Cooking Time: 0 minutes

Servings: 6

Ingredients:

1 bunch kale

1 pound Brussels sprouts

¼ cup craisins (or dry cranberries)

½ cup pecans, chopped

Maple vinaigrette:

½ cup olive oil

¼ cup apple cider vinegar

¼ cup maple syrup

1 teaspoon dry mustard

Directions:

Slice the kale and Brussels sprouts with a cheese grater or mandolin slicer. Transfer to a salad bowl.

Add the pecans to a skillet on high heat. Toast for 60 seconds, then transfer to the salad bowl.

Add the craisins.

Mix all of the ingredients for the vinaigrette and whisk to combine.

Pour the vinaigrette over the salad and toss. Refrigerate for a few hours or preferably overnight before serving.

Tomato, Cucumber and Onion Salad

Preparation Time: 5 minutes

Cooking Time: 0 minutes

Servings: 6

Ingredients:

1 pound grape tomatoes

3 cucumbers, sliced

½ cup white onion, sliced thinly

1 cup white vinegar

2 tablespoons Italian dressing

½ cup sugar

Directions:

Whisk together the vinegar, sugar, and Italian dressing in a small bowl.

Add the cucumbers, tomatoes, and onions. Toss to coat. Cover with plastic wrap and refrigerate until ready to serve or for at least 1 hour before serving.

Roasted Tomato Sauce

Preparation time: 2 hours

Cooking time: 75 minutes

Servings: 4

Ingredients:

1 1/2 kilos of tomatoes

3 tablespoon extra-virgin olive oil

6 peeled garlic cloves

1/2 cup sliced onion

2 teaspoons Italian seasoning

1 teaspoon kosher salt

1/4 teaspoon freshly ground black pepper

3 tablespoons chopped basil

Optional: 2 tablespoons tomato paste

Optional: 500 g of pasta

Optional: 1/8 teaspoon chopped red pepper flakes

Directions:

Gather the ingredients of the roasted tomato sauce and preheat the oven to 150 ºC.

Wash the tomatoes, remove the stem and cut them into pieces of approximately 2 centimeters.

Mix the tomatoes in a large bowl with olive oil, sliced onion, rolled garlic cloves, Italian seasoning, salt, and ground black pepper.

Place the tomatoes in a single layer on a baking sheet and bake for 60 minutes. Put roasted tomatoes and condiments in a food processor or blender.

Mix well and transfer to a large saucepan and add chopped basil, red peppers, and tomato paste, if you use them. Bring the roasted tomato sauce over low heat, and cook for 15 minutes or until reduced and thickened.

Cook the pasta in boiling water with salt; drains Mix the drained hot pasta with the sauce and serve with garlic bread if you wish.

If you are not going to use the sauce immediately, place it in a container or in glass jars with a lid and refrigerate and consume for up to 3 days, or store it in the freezer for up to 4 months.

Chapter 4: Pasta

Pesto Chicken and Broccoli Pasta

Preparation Time: 15 minutes

Cooking Time: 30 minutes

Servings: 4

Ingredients:

4 cups cooked pasta

½ onion, minced

4 garlic cloves, minced

¼ cup pesto

2 chicken breasts; sliced into ½" strips

1 cup half and half or light cream

¼ cup parmesan cheese, grated

1 cup broccoli florets, fresh or frozen

¼ teaspoon pepper or to taste

1 tablespoon olive oil

½ teaspoon salt

Directions:

Cook the pasta in a large pot per the directions mentioned on the package. During the last one minute of your cooking; add broccoli into the pot with pasta. Drain & set aside until ready to use.

In the meantime, over moderate heat in a large pan; heat 1 tablespoon of oil. Add and cook the onion until turn golden, for 3 to 4 minutes. Add and cook the garlic for a couple of seconds and then add the sliced chicken. Season with pepper & salt; cook until the chicken turn browned, for 5 to 7 minutes.

Add the cream, parmesan, pesto, pepper & salt. Let the mixture to simmer for 2 to 3 minutes. Add the cooked broccoli and pasta. Give the ingredients a good stir until completely combined. Let simmer for 2 to 3 more minutes. Remove from heat & garnish with additional parmesan. Serve hot & enjoy.

Cheesecake Factory's Pasta di Vinci

Preparation Time: 10 minutes
Cooking Time: 50 minutes
Servings: 4

Ingredients:

½ red onion, chopped

1 cup mushrooms, quartered

2 teaspoons garlic, chopped

1-pound chicken breast, cut into bite-size pieces

3 tablespoons butter, divided

2 tablespoons flour

2 teaspoons salt

¼ cup white wine

1 cup cream of chicken soup mixed with some milk

4 tablespoons heavy cream

Basil leaves for serving, chopped

Parmesan cheese for serving

1 pound penne pasta, cooked, drained

Directions:

Sauté the onion, mushrooms and garlic in 1 tablespoon of the butter.

When they are tender, remove them from the butter and place in a bowl. Cook the chicken in the same pan.

When the chicken is done, transfer it to the bowl containing the garlic, onions, and mushrooms, and set everything aside.

Using the same pan, make a roux using the flour and remaining butter over low to medium heat. When the roux is ready, mix in the salt, wine, and cream of chicken mixture. Continue stirring the mixture, making sure that it does not burn.

When the mixture thickens, allow the mixture to simmer for a few more minutes.

Mix in the ingredients that you set aside and transfer the cooked pasta to a bowl or plate.

Pour the sauce over the pasta, garnish with parmesan cheese and basil, and serve.

Olive Garden Angry Alfredo with Chicken

Preparation Time: 10 minutes

Cooking time: 30 minutes

Servings: 8

Ingredients for Sauce:

Four ounces of butter

One cup heavy cream

Half cup freshly grated Parmesan cheese

Half teaspoon garlic powder

Quarter tsp red pepper chili flakes For Chicken

8 ounces chicken breast salt and pepper

1 tablespoon olive oil Top with

1/2 cup Mozzarella cheese

Directions:

In 8 ounces of Chicken breast, add salt and pepper, add one tablespoon olive oil. Add the heavy cream, and then add the cheese and stir until the sauce thickens until it starts to bubble. Lower the temperature to simmer. Add the crushed red peppers and ground garlic.

The chicken is flavored with salt and pepper. Preferably an iron skillet over medium-high heat in a medium-sized pan and add a few tablespoons of olive oil.

For five to seven minutes cook the chicken or cook until the chicken edges start turning white, flip the chicken breast over and continue cooking until finished. The chicken will cook for another 5 to 7 minutes.

Preheat the grill over your oven. Enable the chicken to lie down for a few minutes, then slice into pieces of bite-size. Combine the Chicken and the Alfredo sauce. Layer in a quarter saucepan. Cover with cheese made from mozzarella.

Place the saucepan under the broiler and let the cheese brown.

When the cheese from Mozzarella just starts brown, remove from the oven.

Chow Mein from Panda Express

Preparation Time: 5 minutes
Cooking Time: 30 minutes
Servings: 6

Ingredients:

8 quarts water

12 ounces Yakisoba noodles

¼ cup soy sauce

3 garlic cloves, finely chopped

1 tablespoon brown sugar

2 teaspoons ginger, grated

¼ teaspoon white pepper, ground

2 tablespoons olive oil

1 onion, finely chopped

3 celery stalks, sliced on the bias

2 cups cabbage, chopped

Directions:

In a pot, bring water to a boil. Cook Yakisoba noodles for about 1 minute until noodles separate. Drain and set aside.

Combine soy sauce, garlic, brown sugar, ginger, and white pepper in a bowl.

In a pan, heat oil on medium-high heat. Sauté onion and celery for 3 minutes or until soft. Add cabbage and stir-fry for an additional minute. Mix in noodles and soy sauce mixture. Cook for 2 minutes, stirring continuously until noodles are well-coated.

Transfer into bowls. Serve.

Pesto Cavatappi from Noodles & Company

Preparation Time: 5 minutes
Cooking Time: 20 minutes
Servings: 8

Ingredients:

4 quarts water

1 tablespoon salt

1-pound macaroni pasta

1 teaspoon olive oil

1 large tomato, finely chopped

4 ounces mushrooms, finely chopped

¼ cup chicken broth

¼ cup dry white wine

¼ cup heavy cream

1 cup pesto

1 cup Parmesan cheese, grated

Directions:

Add water and salt to a pot. Bring to a boil. Put in pasta and cook for 10 minutes or until al dente. Drain and set aside.

In a pan, heat oil. Sauté tomatoes and mushrooms for 5 minutes. Pour in broth, wine, and cream. Bring to a boil. Reduce heat to medium and simmer for 2 minutes or until mixture is thick. Stir in pesto and cook for another 2 minutes. Toss in pasta. Mix until fully coated.

Transfer onto plates and sprinkle with Parmesan cheese.

Chapter 5: Chicken

Chicken Pot Pie

Preparation Time: 5 minutes

Cooking Time: 30 minutes

Servings: 6

Ingredients:

½ cup butter

1 medium onion, diced

1 (14.5-ounce) can chicken broth

1 cup half and half milk

½ cup all-purpose flour

1 carrot, diced

1 celery stalk, diced

3 medium potatoes, peeled and diced

3 cups cooked chicken, diced

½ cup frozen peas

1 teaspoon chicken seasoning

½ teaspoon salt

½ teaspoon ground pepper

1 single refrigerated pie crust

1 egg

Water

Directions:

Preheat the oven to 375°F.

In a large skillet, heat the butter over medium heat, add the leeks and sauté for 3 minutes.

Sprinkle flour over the mixture and continue to stir constantly for 3 minutes.

Whisking constantly, blend in the chicken broth and milk. Bring the mixture to a boil. Reduce heat to medium-low.

Add the carrots, celery, potatoes, salt, pepper, and stir to combine. Cook for 10-15 minutes or until veggies are cooked through but still crisp. Add chicken and peas. Stir to combine.

Transfer chicken filling to a deep 9-inch pie dish.

Fit the pie crust sheet on top and press the edges around the dish to seal the crust. Trim the excess if needed.

In a separate bowl, whisk an egg with 1 tablespoon of water, and brush the mixture over the top of the pie. With a knife, cut a few slits to let steam escape.

Bake the pie in the oven on the middle oven rack 20 to 30 minutes until the crust becomes golden brown.

Let the pie rest for about 15 minutes before serving.

Green Chili Jack Chicken

Preparation Time: 5 minutes

Cooking Time: 30 minutes

Servings: 6

Ingredients:

1-pound chicken strips

1 teaspoon chili powder

4 ounces green chilies

2 cups Monterey Jack cheese, shredded

¼ cup salsa

Directions:

Sprinkle the chicken with the chili powder while heating some oil over medium heat.

Cook the chicken strips until they are half cooked, and then place the green chilies on top of the chicken. Lower the heat to low.

Cook for 1 to 2 minutes before adding the cheese on top. Keep cooking the chicken and cheese until the cheese melts.

Serve the chicken with the salsa.

Cracker Barrel Chicken Potpie

Preparation Time: 5 minutes
Cooking Time: 30 minutes
Servings: 6

Ingredients:

Two tablespoons canola oil

One medium onion, chopped

1/2 cup all-purpose flour

One teaspoon poultry seasoning

3/4 cup 2% milk

One can (14-1/2 ounces) chicken broth

3 cups cubed cooked chicken

2 cups of frozen mixed vegetables, thawed

One sheet refrigerated pie crust

Directions:

Preheat the oven to 450 ° C. Heat oil in a large saucepan over medium-high heat. Add onion; stir and cook until tender. Season with flour and poultry until blended; whisk slowly in broth and milk. Shift to 9-inch grained deep-soaked pie plate; place the crust over the filling. Trim and seal the edges. In the crust put some slits. Bake for 15-20 minutes or until golden brown.

Double Chicken Pie

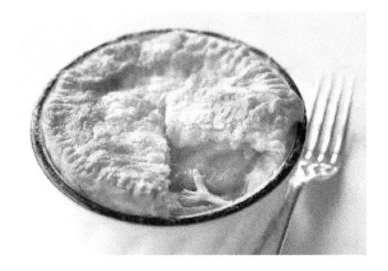

Preparation Time: 5 minutes

Cooking Time: 30 minutes

Servings: 6

Ingredients:

½ cup butter

1 medium onion, diced

1 (14.5-ounce) can chicken broth

1 cup half and half milk

½ cup all-purpose flour

1 carrot, diced

1 celery stalk, diced

3 medium potatoes, peeled and diced

3 cups cooked chicken, diced

½ cup frozen peas

1 teaspoon chicken seasoning

½ teaspoon salt

½ teaspoon ground pepper

1 single refrigerated pie crust

1 egg

Water

Directions:

Preheat the oven to 375°F.

In a large skillet, heat the butter over medium heat, add the leeks and sauté for 3 minutes.

Sprinkle flour over the mixture, and continue to stir constantly for 3 minutes.

Whisking constantly, blend in the chicken broth and milk. Bring the mixture to a boil. Reduce heat to medium-low.

Add the carrots, celery, potatoes, salt, pepper, and stir to combine. Cook for 10-15 minutes or until veggies are cooked through but still crisp. Add chicken and peas. Stir to combine.

Transfer chicken filling to a deep 9-inch pie dish.

Fit the pie crust sheet on top and press the edges around the dish to seal the crust. Trim the excess if needed.

In a separate bowl, whisk an egg with 1 tablespoon of water, and brush the mixture over the top of the pie. With a knife, cut a few slits to let steam escape.

Bake the pie in the oven on the middle oven rack 20 to 30 minutes until the crust becomes golden brown.

Let the pie rest for about 15 minutes before serving.

Grilled Chicken Tenderloin

Preparation Time: 10 min.

Marinating time 1 hour

Cooking time: 30 min.

Servings: 4–5

Ingredients:

4–5 boneless and skinless chicken breasts, cut into strips, or 12 chicken tenderloins, tendons removed

1 cup Italian dressing

2 teaspoons lime juice

4 teaspoons honey

Directions:

Combine the dressing, lime juice and honey in a plastic bag. Seal and shake to combine.

Place the chicken in the bag. Seal and shake again, then transfer to the refrigerator for at least 1 hour. The longer it marinates, the more the flavors will infuse into the chicken.

When ready to prepare, transfer the chicken and the marinade to a large nonstick skillet.

Bring to a boil, then reduce the heat and allow to simmer until the liquid has cooked down to a glaze.

Chapter 6: Beef and Pork

The Cheesecake Factory Famous Meatloaf

Preparation Time: 10 minutes
Cooking time: 45 minutes
Servings: 8

Meatloaf Ingredients:

¾ cup of breadcrumbs

¾ cup of whole milk

½ teaspoon of paprika

1 teaspoon of ground sage

1 teaspoon of ground black pepper

1 ½ teaspoons of dried thyme

2 teaspoons of salt

1 tablespoon of granulated sugar

1 tablespoon of minced Italian parsley

1 pound of ground pork

1 ½ pounds of ground sirloin

3 eggs, beaten

5 teaspoons of minced garlic

⅓ cup of shredded and minced carrot

½ cup of minced red onion

2 tablespoons of minced red bell pepper

2 tablespoons of minced green bell pepper

1 tablespoon of vegetable oil

Grilled Onion Ingredients:

¼ teaspoon of ground black pepper

¼ teaspoon of salt

2 tablespoons of butter

1 medium sliced onion

Mushroom Gravy Ingredients:

¼ teaspoon of ground sage

¼ teaspoon of dried thyme

¼ teaspoon of ground black pepper

¼ teaspoon of salt

1 teaspoon of minced Italian parsley

1 ½ cups of sliced mushrooms

2 tablespoons of all-purpose flour

1 14-ounce can of beef broth

1 teaspoon of minced garlic

2 tablespoons of garlic

Directions:

1) Prepare your oven by preheating it to 350 degrees F.

2) Take a medium sauté pan and place it over medium-low heat with a tablespoon of oil in it. Slowly sauté the minced red and green bell peppers for about 5 minutes. Add minced garlic, onion, and carrot and cook for 5 more minutes, just to get these veggies softened.

3) Take a large bowl and whisk the eggs in it. Add the ground pork, beef, sautéed veggies, and all the other ingredients, but leave out the breadcrumbs. Manually mix all the ingredients until everything is blended, then sprinkle some breadcrumbs in a little bit at a time. Place the meatloaf into a 9-x 5-inch loaf pan and bake it in the oven for about an hour. Take the meatloaf out of the oven and let it chill for about 30 minutes.

4) In the meantime, you can grill the onions while the meatloaf cools. Place butter in a medium sauté pan over medium-low heat, then add onions, pepper, and salt, and cook for about 20 to 25 minutes and stir constantly until the onions turn light brown.

5) To prepare the gravy, take a pan, place butter in it over medium-low heat, let it melt, then add garlic and sauté it for 1 minute. Add flour, cook for 2 to 3 minutes while whisking constantly until the mixture is light brown. Add the rest of the ingredients and simmer for 10 to 15 minutes or until the sauce gets thicker.

6) To serve the meatloaf, you will need to preheat the broiler to high first. Take the meatloaf from the loaf pan and slice it into nine 1-inch-thick slices. Put the slices

on a baking sheet, and place them under the broiler for about 2 to 3 minutes, until the meatloaf slices are hot.

7) Put the slices of meatloaf on a serving plate, pour gravy over them and top with grilled onions. Enjoy!

Tip: Be sure to use both pork and sirloin for the best flavor.

Denny's Country Fried Steak

Preparation Time: 10 minutes **Cooking time: 50 minutes** **Servings: 8**

Ingredients:

1 pound beef cube steak, dice into 4 pieces

½ cup buttermilk

1 teaspoon salt

1 cup flour

½ teaspoon paprika

½ teaspoon pepper

¼ cup vegetable oil

Directions:

1. Make the meat tender by beating it with a mallet or the bottom of a heavy skillet.

2. In a shallow dish, stir the flour, salt, paprika and pepper together. 3. Place the buttermilk in a separate platter.

4. Dredge steaks in the flour mixture, dip in buttermilk and dip in the flour mixture again.

5. Heat up oil over medium-high heat in a large skillet.

6. Cook the steaks on either side for 5 minutes.

7. Serve with Denny's Country Gravy, if preferred.

Chili's Baby Back Ribs

Preparation Time: 5 minutes
Cooking Time: 30 minutes
Servings: 6

Ingredients Pork:

4 racks baby-back pork ribs

Sauce:

1½ cups water

1 cup white vinegar

½ cup tomato paste

1 tablespoon yellow mustard

⅔ cup dark brown sugar packed

1 teaspoon hickory flavored liquid smoke

1½ teaspoons salt

½ teaspoon onion powder

¼ teaspoon garlic powder

¼ teaspoon paprika

Directions:

Mix together all of the sauce ingredients and then bring to a boil.

When the sauce starts to boil, reduce it to a simmer. Continue simmering the mixture for 45 to 60 minutes, mixing occasionally. When the sauce is almost done, preheat the oven to 300°F.

Choose a flat surface and lay some aluminum foil over it, enough to cover 1 rack of ribs. Place the ribs on top.

Remove the sauce from heat and start brushing it all over the ribs.

When the rack is completely covered, wrap it with the aluminum foil and place it on the baking pan with the opening of the foil facing upwards.

Repeat steps 3 to 5 for the remaining racks.

Bake the ribs for 2½ hours.

When they are almost done baking, preheat your grill to medium heat.

Grill both sides of each rack for 4 to 8 minutes. When you are almost done grilling, brush some more sauce over each side and grill for a few more minutes. Make sure that the sauce doesn't burn.

Transfer the racks to a large plate and serve with extra sauce.

Applebee's Honey Barbecue Sauce with Riblets

Preparation Time: 5 minutes

Cooking Time: 30 minutes

Servings: 6

Ingredients:

Honey Barbecue Sauce

1 cup ketchup

½ cup corn syrup

½ cup honey

¼ cup apple cider vinegar

¼ cup water

2 tablespoons molasses

2 teaspoons dry mustard

2 teaspoons garlic powder

1 teaspoon chili powder

1 teaspoon onion powder

Meat:

2¼ pounds pork riblets

Salt

Pepper

Garlic

¼ teaspoon liquid smoke flavoring

1 teaspoon water

Directions:

Season the riblets with the salt, garlic, and pepper based on your preferences, then sear them on a grill until the meat starts to separate from the bone. While doing this, preheat the oven to 275°F.

Mix the water and liquid smoke flavoring into a deep pan and place the ribs on an elevated rack inside—make sure that the liquid does not touch the ribs.

Cover the pan with two layers of foil and bake for 2 to 5 hours, depending on the strength of your oven and the number of riblets you have. Make sure that the internal temperature of the meat reaches 155°F all throughout.

While waiting for the riblets to cook, prepare the sauce by mixing all of the sauce ingredients together and simmering for 20 minutes.

When the sauce is done cooking, transfer to a bowl and set aside.

When the ribs are done cooking, sear them on a grill until the marrow starts sizzling.

Place the ribs on a plate and cover generously with the sauce.

Serve and enjoy.

Stuffed Pork Chop

Preparation Time: 15 minutes
Cooking Time: 3 hours 30 minutes
Serving: 4

Ingredients:

8 pork chops

½ pound sausages

2 cups rice, cooked

1 tablespoon chopped celery leaves

1 tablespoon sausage drippings

1 tablespoon chopped parsley

1 small onion, grated

1 teaspoon poultry seasoning

½ teaspoon salt

⅛ teaspoon pepper

Directions:

Preheat the oven to 350°F.

Slice each pork chop on one side to create a pocket.

Combine the cooked rice, sausage, celery leaves, sausage drippings, parsley, onion, poultry seasoning, salt, and pepper in a bowl and stir well.

Stuff the mixture into the pockets you created in the pork chops.

Bake, covered, for about 1½–2 hours.

About 15 minutes before the chops are done, remove the cover to allow them to brown on top.

Chapter 7: Fish and Seafood

Feta Shrimp Skillet

Preparation Time: 15 minutes

Cooking Time: 40 minutes

Serving: 4

Ingredients:

1/3 cup finely chopped onion

1-1/2 teaspoons olive oil

Two garlic cloves, minced

One can (14-1/2 ounces) diced tomatoes, undrained

Two tablespoons white wine, optional

1/2 teaspoon dried oregano

1/4 teaspoon pepper

1/8 teaspoon salt

1/2-pound uncooked medium shrimp, deveined and peeled

One tablespoon minced fresh parsley

Six tablespoons crumbled feta cheese

Directions:

Saute onion in oil until tender, in a large nonstick skillet.

Remove Garlic and cook for 1 minute. Stir in the tomatoes, sugar, oregano, pepper, and salt if desired. Take to a simmer.

Reduce heat; simmer, expose, for 5-7 minutes or until sauce thickens slightly.

Stir in parsley and shrimps.

Cook and stir for 5-6 minutes over medium heat or until shrimp turns pink.

From heat remove, sprinkle with cheese.

Cover and let stand for 5-10 minutes, or until it softens the cheese.

Salmon gravlax

Preparation Time: 15 minutes

Cooking Time: 30 minutes

Serving: 4

Ingredients:

2 salmon fillets of 1 kilo each, without skin

¼ cup vodka

1/3 cup fine sea salt

1/3 cup sugar

1 tablespoon ground black pepper

¼ cup chopped dill

Direction:

Gather the ingredients of salmon gravlax.

Rinse the salmon fillets and dry them well.

Use pliers or pliers to remove the spines if necessary.

Sprinkle the salmon evenly with the vodka.

In a small bowl combine sugar, fine sea salt and ground black pepper.

Divide the mixture into three equal parts inside the bowl.

Put half of the one-third of the curing mixture on a rimmed baking sheet.

Place a skinless salmon fillet on the mixture and spread a third in the mixture on the fillet.

Spread the other half of the third over the second steak and sprinkle both with chopped dill.

Place the second fillet on the first and sprinkle the remaining curing mixture on the skin of the upper salmon.

Cover the tray with foil and place a wooden board on the covered fish. Cover with a heavy pot and bring it to the refrigerator for at least 12 hours.

Remove from the refrigerator and discard the accumulated liquid in the tray. Bring the salmon back in the refrigerator for 12 hours.

Its fish is already cured and you can serve it, but it will continue to benefit from another 12 to 24 hours of refrigeration.

Chi-Chi's Seafood Chimichanga

Preparation Time: 15 minutes

Cooking Time: 30 minutes

Serving: 4

Ingredients:

4 tablespoons butter

4 tablespoons flour

½ teaspoon butter

2 dashes black pepper, ground

2 cups milk

8 ounces jack cheese, shredded

1 16-ounce package crab meat, flaked

1 cup cottage cheese

¼ cup Parmesan cheese

1 egg

1 tablespoon dried parsley flakes

¼ teaspoon onion powder

1 tablespoon lemon juice

Shredded lettuce for serving

¼ cup sliced green onions for garnish

Directions:

Preheat oven to 375°F.

To make the sauce, heat butter in a pan on medium heat. Add flour, salt, and pepper. Mix, then pour in milk. Stirring often, cook until sauce is thick then simmer for an additional 1 minute.

Turn off heat and stir in jack cheese until completely blended into sauce.

In a bowl, combine crab meat, cottage and Parmesan cheese, egg, parsley, and onion powder. Heat tortillas in microwave for 10 seconds or until warm. Wet bottom side of tortilla and add crab meat mixture on top. Fold tortilla to wrap filling.

Coat baking sheet with cooking spray. Bake chimichangas for about 25 minutes.

Reheat sauce until warm. Mix in lemon juice and stir until blended.

Transfer chimichangas to plates over a bed of shredded lettuce, if desired. Top with sauce and garnish with green onions before serving.

Red Lobster's Copycat Lobster Pizza

Preparation Time: 15 minutes

Cooking Time: 30 minutes

Serving: 4

Ingredients:

1 10-inch flour tortillas

1 ounce roasted garlic butter

2 tablespoons Parmesan cheese, shredded

1/2 cup fresh Roma tomatoes, finely chopped

2 tablespoons fresh basil, cut into thin strips

2 ounces lobster meat, chopped

½ cup Italian cheese blend, grated

Vegetable oil for coating

Dash salt and pepper

Fresh lemon juice for serving

Directions:

Preheat oven to 450°F.

Coat one side of tortilla with garlic butter. Top with Parmesan cheese, tomatoes, basil, lobster meat, and Italian cheese blend in that order. Set aside.

Prepare a pizza pan. Apply a light coat of vegetable oil and cover with a dash of salt and pepper. Transfer pizza onto pan. Bake for about 5 minutes.

Cut into slices and drizzle with lemon juice. Serve.

Tilapia Florentine

Preparation Time: 15 minutes

Cooking Time: 30 minutes

Serving: 4

Ingredients:

One package (6 ounces) fresh baby spinach

Six teaspoons canola oil, divided

Four tilapia fillets (4 ounces each)

One egg, lightly beaten

2 tablespoons lime juice

Two teaspoons garlic-herb seasoning blend

1/4 cup grated Parmesan cheese

1/2 cup part-skim ricotta cheese

Directions:

Cook the spinach in 4 teaspoons of oil until wilted in a large nonstick skillet; drain. In the meantime, put tilapia in a fattened 13-in. x in 9. Baking platter. Drizzle with remaining lime juice and oil. Sprinkle with a blend to season.

Combine the egg, ricotta cheese and spinach in a small bowl; spoon filets over. Sprinkle with a cheese made with Parmesan.

Bake for 15-20 minutes at 375 °, or quickly with a fork until the fish flakes.

Chapter 8: Vegetarian

Corn Cream Recipe

Preparation Time: 15 minutes

Cooking Time: 30 minutes

Serving: 4

Ingredients:

1 ear of corn

1 yellow pepper

1 onion

1 tablespoon butter

1 splash of cream

Vegetable soup

1 dash of extra virgin olive oil

Directions:

Place the butter in a pan and brown the previously peeled and finely chopped onion.

When the onion is transparent, add the yellow pepper cut into small cubes along with the corn and a drizzle of extra virgin olive oil.

114

When the vegetables are golden brown, cover with the vegetable stock.

Crush the preparation with a splash of cream or milk and serve the hot corn cream. Garnish with corn kernels and chopped parsley.

Chipotle Baba Ghanoush

Preparation Time: 10 minutes

Cooking Time: 30 minutes

Servings: 6

Ingredients:

3 pounds eggplants; sliced in half

1 teaspoon garlic, minced

¼ teaspoon chipotle powder for dip plus more to sprinkle on top

2 tablespoons tahini sesame seed paste

1 ½ teaspoon olive oil

2 tablespoons lemon juice, freshly squeezed

1 teaspoon kosher salt

Directions:

Preheat your oven to 350F in advance. Place eggplant on a large-sized baking sheet sprayed with nonstick spray or lined with parchment paper, flesh-side down.

Bake the eggplants until the flesh is soft, for 30 minutes. Let the eggplants to cool until you can easily handle them. Scrape the meat of the eggplant into a medium-sized bowl; discarding the skins. Add tahini, minced garlic, olive oil, lemon juice, chipotle powder & kosher salt; mix well.

Pour into a serving dish & drizzle with more of olive oil & sprinkle some more chipotle powder, if desired. Enjoy.

Chopped Caprese Salad-Vero Amore

Cooking Time: 10 minutes

Preparation time: 10 minutes

Serving time: 8

Ingredients:

5 heirloom tomatoes

8 broad leaves of basil

1 Eight oz tub of ciliegine mozzarella balls

1 or 2 tablespoons of olive oil

4 tablespoon balsamic vinegar salt & pepper to taste

Directions:

Dice the tomatoes.

Chop in thin slices of the basil.

Attach the mozzarella, onions, and basil to a large bowl or platter.

Season to balsamic vinegar with salt and pepper and drizzle.

Boston Market's Squash Casserole

Preparation	Time:	15	minutes
Cooking Time: 30 minutes			
Serving: 4			

Ingredients:

Vegetable oil for coating

1 8½-ounce box corn muffin mix

4½ cup zucchini, finely chopped

4½ cup summer squash, finely chopped

⅓ cup butter

1½ cups yellow onion, minced

1 teaspoon salt

½ teaspoon black pepper, ground

½ teaspoon thyme

1 tablespoon fresh parsley, sliced

2 chicken bouillon cubes

1 teaspoon garlic, finely chopped

8 ounces cheddar cheese, chopped

Directions:

Preheat oven to 350°F and lightly coat baking tray with vegetable oil.

Follow package instructions to cook corn muffins. Set aside.

In a deep pan, add zucchini and summer squash. Pour water into pan, enough to cover vegetables. Simmer over medium-low heat or until vegetables are soft. Add cooked squash mixture into a container along with 1 cup of the cooking water. Reserve for later. Discard remaining liquids.

Return pan to heat. Melt butter, then stir-fry onions until fragrant. Add salt, pepper, thyme, and parsley. Stir in chicken bouillon cubes, garlic, cooked squash and zucchini mixture, and cheese. Sprinkle with crumbled corn muffins. Stir everything together until well-blended, then pour onto baking tray and cover with tinfoil.

Cook in oven for about 40 minutes. Remove cover and bake for an additional 20 minutes.

Serve hot.

DIY Sweet Potato Casserole from Ruth's Chris

Preparation Time: 15 minutes

Cooking Time: 30 minutes

Serving: 4

Ingredients:

2 large sweet potatoes covered in aluminum foil

⅓ cup plus 3 tablespoons butter, divided

2 tablespoons half and half

Salt, to taste

½ cup brown sugar

¼ cup all-purpose flour

1 cup pecans, diced

Directions:

Preheat oven to 350°F.

Place sweet potatoes onto a baking tray and bake for about 60 minutes. Remove from oven.

In a bowl, add baked sweet potatoes, 3 tablespoons butter, half and half, and salt. Mash until well blended. In a separate bowl, combine pecans, brown sugar, flour, and remaining butter.

Transfer mashed sweet potatoes into a casserole dish, then top with pecan mixture. Place in oven and bake for about 20 minutes until edges bubble and pecan topping is slightly brown.

Serve.

Chapter 9: Bread and Soups

Olive Garden Italian Sausage Soup

Preparation Time: 15 minutes

Cooking Time: 30 minutes

Serving: 4

Ingredients:

1 pound ground sweet Italian sausage

¼ teaspoon ground black pepper

1 (10¾-ounce) can tomatoes

1 cup white rice

1 (10-ounce) box thawed and drained chopped spinach

6 cups beef broth

Romano cheese, for garnish

Directions:

1. Cook the sausage over medium heat in a soup pot for 10-12 minutes. Split the beef as it heats, using a fork.

2. Tomatoes, rice, broth and black pepper are then added. Bring the pot to a boil.

3. Cook for 12-15 minutes, or until the rice is tender.

4. Remove the chopped spinach and allow to simmer for a few minutes.

5. Ladle in bowls soup, and garnish with cheese.

PF Chang's Spicy Chicken Noodle Soup

Preparation Time: 15 minutes

Cooking Time: 15 minutes

Servings: 4-6

Ingredients:

2 quarts chicken stock

1 tablespoon granulated sugar

3 tablespoons white vinegar

2 cloves garlic, minced

1 tablespoon ginger, freshly minced

¼ cup soy sauce

Sriracha sauce to taste

Red pepper flakes to taste

1-pound boneless chicken breast, cut into thin 2–3 inch pieces

3 tablespoons cornstarch

Salt to taste

1 cup mushrooms, sliced

1 cup grape tomatoes, halved

3 green onions, sliced

2 tablespoons fresh cilantro, chopped

½ pound pasta, cooked to just under package directions and drained

Directions:

Add the chicken stock, sugar, vinegar, garlic, ginger, soy sauce, Sriracha and red pepper flakes to a large saucepan. Bring to a boil, then lower the heat to a simmer. Let cook for 5 minutes.

Season chicken with salt to taste. In a resealable bag, combine the chicken and the cornstarch. Shake to coat.

Add the chicken to the simmering broth a piece at a time. Then add the mushrooms. Continue to cook for another 5 minutes.

Stir in the tomatoes, green onions, cilantro, and cooked pasta.

Serve with additional cilantro.

Chili's Chili

Preparation Time: 10 minutes

Cooking Time: 1 hour and 10 minutes

Servings: 8

Ingredients:

For Chili:

4 pounds ground chuck - ground for chili

1 ½ cups yellow onions, chopped

16 ounces tomato sauce

1 tablespoon cooking oil

3 ¼ plus 1 cups water

1 tablespoon masa harina

For Chili Spice Blend:

1 tablespoon paprika

½ cup chili powder

1 teaspoon ground black pepper

1/8 cup ground cumin

1 teaspoon cayenne pepper or to taste

1/8 cup salt

1 teaspoon garlic powder

Directions:

Combine the entire chili spice ingredients together in a small bowl; continue to combine until thoroughly mixed.

Now, over moderate heat in a 6-quart stock pot; place & cook the meat until browned; drain. In the meantime; combine the chili spice mix together with tomato sauce & 3 ¼ cups of water in the bowl; give the ingredients a good stir until blended well.

Add the chili seasoning liquid to the browned meat; give it a good stir & bring the mixture to a boil over moderate heat.

Over medium heat in a large skillet; heat 1 tablespoon of the cooking oil & sauté the onions until translucent, for a couple of minutes. Add the sautéed onions to the chili.

Decrease the heat to low & let simmer for an hour, stirring after every 10 to 15 minutes. Combine the masa harina with the leftover water in a separate bowl; mix well. Add to the chili stock pot & cook for 10 more minutes.

Chicken Enchilada Soup

Preparation Time: 10 minutes

Cooking Time: 15 minutes

Servings: 10

Ingredients:

2 rotisserie chickens or 3 pounds cooked diced chicken

½ pound processed American cheese; cut in small cubes

3 cups yellow onions, diced

¼ cup chicken base

2 cups masa harina

½ teaspoon cayenne pepper

2 teaspoon granulated garlic

1 - 2 teaspoons salt or to taste

2 cups tomatoes, crushed

½ cup vegetable oil

2 teaspoon chili powder

4 quarts water

2 teaspoon ground cumin

Directions:

Over moderate heat in a large pot; combine oil together with onions, chicken base, granulated garlic, chili powder, cumin, cayenne & salt. Cook for 3 to 5 minutes, until onions are soft & turn translucent, stirring occasionally.

Combine 1 quart of water with masa harina in a large measuring cup or pitcher.

Continue to stir until no lumps remain. Add to the onions; bring the mixture to a boil, over moderate heat.

Once done, cook for a couple of minutes, stirring constantly. Stir in the tomatoes & leftover 3 quarts of water. Bring the soup to a boil again, stirring every now and then. Add in the cheese.

Cook until the cheese is completely melted, stirring occasionally. Add the chicken & cook until heated through. Serve immediately & enjoy.

Olive Garden Pasta Roma Soup

Preparation Time: 15 minutes
Cooking Time: 60 minutes
Serving: 4

Ingredients:

2 (16-ounce) cans drained garbanzo beans

1 cup julienned carrots

1/3 cup olive oil ¾ cup diced onions

¼ teaspoon minced garlic

1 cup diced celery

6 slices cooked bacon

1 quart chicken broth

1½ cups canned drained chopped tomatoes

½ teaspoon black pepper

2 tablespoons chopped fresh parsley

1/8 teaspoon ground rosemary ½ cup cooked macaroni

Directions:

1. Add the beans to a food processor and process until the beans mash properly.

2. Steam up the oil in a large pot. Add the carrots, onions, celery, and garlic and sauté over medium heat for 5 minutes.

3. Add remaining ingredients to the pot except for pasta. Bring this all to a boil. Reduce heat to a simmer and cook, stirring regularly, for 20 minutes.

4. Add the pasta to the finished soup and straight right away.

Chapter 10: Desserts

Chocolate Pecan Pie

Preparation Time: 15 minutes
Cooking Time: 50 minutes
Serving: 4

Ingredients:

3 eggs

½ cup sugar

1 cup corn syrup

½ teaspoon salt

1 teaspoon vanilla extract

¼ cup melted butter

1 cup pecans

3 tablespoons semisweet chocolate chips

1 unbaked pie shell

Directions:

Preheat the oven to 350°F.

Beat together the eggs and sugar in a mixing bowl, then add the corn syrup, salt, vanilla and butter.

Put the chocolate chips and pecans inside the pie shell and pour the egg mixture over the top.

Bake for 50–60 minutes or until set.

Serve with vanilla ice cream.

Starbucks® Mocha Frappuccino

Preparation Time: 10 minutes

Cooking Time: 10 minutes

Servings: 8

Ingredients:

¾ cup chocolate syrup

4 cups milk

¾ cup sugar

3 cups espresso coffee

For Topping:

Chocolate syrup

Whipped cream

Directions:

Prepare the coffee as per the directions provided by the manufacturer.

Mix hot coffee & sugar in a mixer until the sugar is completely dissolved, for a minute or two, on high settings.

Add chocolate syrup & milk; continue to mix for a minute more.

For easy storage, pour the mixture into a sealable container. Store in a refrigerator until ready to use.

Now, combine mix & ice (in equal proportion) in a blender & blend until smooth, on high settings & prepare the drink.

Pour the drink into separate glasses & top each glass first with the whipped cream & then drizzle chocolate syrup on the top.

Serve & enjoy!

New York's Serendipity® Frozen Hot Chocolate

Preparation Time: 10 minutes

Cooking Time: 30 minutes

Servings: 2

Ingredients:

1 tablespoon cocoa powder

2 tablespoons cocoa powder

1/3 cup milk powder, dry, nonfat

1 tablespoon cocoa powder, Hershey's

1/3 cup granulated sugar

1 cup milk

3 cups ice

Pinch of salt

Toppings:

Semisweet chocolate bar shavings (Shave the semisweet chocolate using a carrot peeler)

Whipped cream

Directions:

Combine milk powder together with cocoas, salt & sugar in a medium sized bowl; mix well. Add milk in a blender & then add dry mix & ice. Blend on high settings for a minute or two, until the drink is smooth & the ice is entirely crushed.

Pour everything into large glasses & top it with whipped cream & semisweet chocolate shavings.

Serve & enjoy.

Starbucks' Raspberry Swirl Pound Cake

Preparation Time: 20 minutes

Cooking Time: 60 minutes

Servings: 8

Ingredients:

1 box pound cake mix

¼ cup (½ stick) butter, at room temperature

2 eggs

⅔ cup milk

1 teaspoon lemon juice

⅓ cup raspberry spread

6 drops red food color (optional)

Cream Cheese Frosting

1 (8-ounce) package cream cheese, at room temperature

1 cup powdered sugar

1 teaspoon lemon juice

Directions:

Preheat oven to 350°F. Grease and flour a loaf pan.

Mix cake mix, milk, butter and eggs with an electric mixer, at low speed, until blended (about 30 seconds). Switch speed to medium and mix 2 minutes more.

Pour about ⅓ of the batter into a separate bowl, for the raspberry swirl.

To the original bowl, mix in lemon juice.

To the other bowl, mix in raspberry spread and food color (if using).

Pour about ½ of the white batter into the loaf pan.

Pour about ½ of the raspberry batter on top.

Repeat layering red and white layers.

Cut through the batter with a spatula, lengthwise, to create the swirl.

Bake until just a few crumbs stick to a toothpick inserted at the center (about 55–60 minutes).

Place on a wire rack to cool completely.

Meanwhile, prepare the cream cheese frosting. Cream the cheese using a mixer until fluffy. Mix in powdered sugar to incorporate. Add lemon juice and mix at low speed until smooth.

Frost cooled loaf and serve.

California Pizza Kitchen's Pumpkin Cheesecake

Preparation time: 15 min

Cooking time: 1 h

Servings: 8

Ingredients:

Crust

1½ cups graham cracker crumbs

¼ cup sugar

6 tablespoons unsalted butter, melted

½ teaspoon cinnamon

½ teaspoon ground ginger

Cheesecake:

⅓ cup all-purpose flour

1½ teaspoons ground cinnamon

⅛ teaspoon each ground cardamom, ground cloves, ground ginger and ground nutmeg 3 (8-ounce) packages cream cheese

1½ cups dark brown sugar, packed

1⅛ cups sour cream

3 large eggs

2 teaspoons vanilla extract

1¼ cups canned pumpkin puree

Whipped cream, for garnish

Directions:

Prepare the crust by combining the ingredients until well-blended. You may use a blender or food processor for a finer crust. Press evenly and well into a lined springform pan.

Preheat the oven to 350°F.

For the cheesecake, combine the first 3 (dry) ingredients well and set aside.

Using an electric mixer, beat the cream cheese until softened.

Add sugar and continue beating, scraping sides when needed, until creamy and well-incorporated.

Add the flour mixture and beat until well-blended.

Beat in sour cream.

Drop eggs in one at a time, beating well and scraping down after each addition.

Lastly, add the vanilla and pumpkin puree and beat until well-blended.

Pour mixture into pan with crust.

Bake until center is firm (about 1 hour) or until internal temperature is 180°F.

Place on a wire rack to cool.

Refrigerate overnight to set.

Remove from pan and serve with whipped cream.

Conclusion

If you are a food-driven soul, having a really good meal is one of the great pleasures of life. Such a reward may be even better considering the labor of dining out— making a reservation, getting ready and, of course, settling down to order. But the most magical moment of all is when the long-awaited food arrives–gliding through a crowed dining room and ready to be enjoyed before being put on the table. Including beautifully designed salads and incredibly well crispy, delicious fried all things to silky spaghetti and perfectly cooked steaks— good food for the restaurants always seems to have a little extra to make it show

Now all of this has been possible to do at home, keep delighting your friends with these recipes and keep working out. See you soon with more recipes.

thanks a lot and enjoy!

CPSIA information can be obtained
at www.ICGtesting.com
Printed in the USA
BVHW070859150321
602550BV00010B/1087